The Lie

Exposing the Satanic

Plot Behind

Anti-Semitism

Second Edition

Bruce R. Booker

The Lie

Exposing the Satanic Plot

Behind Anti-Semitism

Second Edition

Bruce R. Booker

Copyright 1993, 2011

Dedication

To my beloved wife Trish, without whose love and support I wouldn't have written this book.

To the Jewish people, from whom came the Messiah Yeshua and our salvation (John 4:22). It is to them that this book is dedicated.

Contents

Foreword

Why is anti-Semitism still around? Why does it know no bounds of geography, time, political entity, religion, or people? What motivates this type of behavior - even across such a widely diverse spectra of humanity?

It is the purpose of this book to expose the true reason behind the continued existence of this hatred towards the Hebrew people. It is hoped that by reading it, a person will become aware of the diabolical plot behind anti-Semitism and take steps to stand against it within their sphere of influence.

It is mainly directed towards Christians because we, of all people are commanded by Jesus to be like the Good Samaritan (Luke 10:30-37) and aid those who are suffering. We are to be the salt of the earth and if we lose our savor, we are good for nothing and should be thrown out to be trampled upon by men (Matthew 5:13).

If we don't speak up, if we remain silent, locked into our own worlds, such as many Christians did in the Holocaust and in the centuries of atrocities towards the Jewish people before it, we will be allowing the Evil one to carry out his plan unopposed. It is our job as believers to fight in the struggle against the spiritual forces of wickedness (Ephesians 6:10-17), not aid and abet the enemy!

"Well, what can I do about it," I am asked, "I'm just one person?"

My Answer: "Use every bit of influence you can muster in your *sphere of influence*. You have friends, relatives, your church leadership, and associates you can influence. You also have a hand to write with, and a mouth to communicate with, so that you can inform your President, your Congressperson, your Senator, or your local government about your position on a particular issue…especially on such an important issue as this. There is much you can do.

So often we feel like, "I'm just one person amongst many in this country" …but even one person plus God is a majority! We lose track of that realization from time-to-time.

Just as Esther was raised, "for such a time as this" (Esther 4:14) and used her influence to save the Jewish people, we must pray that when "such-a-time-as-this" moments come, we will be faithful too.

Even so, God has more "Esthers" in the believing community who feel just as you do. You are not alone. There are many others who have not bowed their knee to the world system.

Read the story about Elijah (1 Kings 19:9-18) who thought that he was alone in his stand for the Lord, only to discover that God had reserved 7,000 who had not bowed their knees to Baal! Perhaps the reason why you feel so alone is because you haven't talked to any of them lately to see if they feel the same as you do about a particular issue of consequence!

I wish to exhort you all, brethren, to stand up now before it is too late! Don't wait for another Holocaust to occur before you say, "Perhaps I should have said something before now!"

Please join with other believers in the fight against the Evil one and his devices – that's what being a believer is all about. And may God richly bless you as you stand on His side, no matter how unpopular it is!

Chapter One

Instigating the Lie

There is a dark shadow looming on the horizon of human existence; it is the lie of anti-Semitism. From time-to-time it blends seemingly into the background and you almost think that it is gone...but it is still there, its wispy tentacles of death reaching out to grasp yet another victim – if it could. Like a chameleon it changes color to suit its environment. In one group of people it appears as a religious cause; in another, a duty to free humanity of a pest that has persisted throughout the millennia.

Yet, whatever its color this sinister lie knows no bounds of time, nationality, race or border; it crosses them all like a menacing cloud over the earth. It sweeps into its vortex its victims, throwing their lifeless bodies into the insidious, hungry flames of the holocaust as though they were nothing but meaningless debris.

Sadly, in its wake, this dark evil lie has resulted in the deaths of untold millions of innocent people throughout the millennia – men, women and children. Whatever its guise, and however "noble" the cause, it nevertheless results from the same satanically inspired prejudice that a group of people that is perceived to be different is somehow inferior to another group.

"Look at *them*. You can tell *them* by their eyes (noses, hair, color, etc.). *They* are to blame for our poor economy (unemployment, deficit, world situation, defeat in the war, etc.). What shall we do with *them*? *They* should be shipped off to where *they* belong (another city, country, concentration camp, etc.). We should not allow *them* to be around our children (wives, property, etc.). We need to do something about *them* now!"

Perhaps every group of people has at one time or another been placed in the role of perpetrator or victim. I recall in American history how the Chinese, the Irish, the Polish, and other people-groups have been persecuted when they came to America. However, that persecution was generally limited to ethnic jokes, ridicule, and ostracism. It didn't include genocide. Yet, no group has been placed into the victim's role as often or as long as the Jewish people who have many times faced those who would see their total destruction.

Since the time in Egypt when a pharaoh arose who "knew not Joseph" (Exodus 1:8 KJV) to the present day, the descendants of Abraham, Isaac and Jacob have been thrust into the role of victim more often and much longer than any other group of people upon the face of the earth.

Each time it happened, the reason was based upon a lie: "The Hebrew people are this and that and we must do something about them." That is not the true motive behind the lie, but simply the surface manifestation of the untruth. There is something much deeper than that, something with a sinister motive so subtle that even the perpetrators might not recognize its origins and purpose. This book was written to expose the real purpose and motive of the lie.

Many throughout the ages have tried to ignore the lie as though it would somehow go away if left alone to itself. They withdraw into their own little worlds as if to say, "Well, so what? It doesn't affect me, so why should I care?"

It is to them that the words of the late German Protestant pastor Martin Niemoller hold the red flag of warning:

First they came for the communists,
and I didn't speak out because I wasn't a
communist.

Then they came for the trade unionists,
and I didn't speak out because I wasn't a trade
unionist.

Then they came for the Jews,
and I didn't speak out because I wasn't a Jew.

Then they came for me
and there was no one left to speak out for me.[1]

"All that is necessary for the triumph of evil is for good men to do nothing"[2] said Edmund Burke. Though it does not affect you now, it one day will. All you have to do is sit there and wait. One day, you too may be declared un-necessary or inferior by another group who is in power. Who will defend you or your family then? So you want to wait until then?

Hitler would not have come to power if the people had stood up against him years before. Even if he

[1] Allan Gould, *What did They Think of the Jews?* Northvale, NJ: Jason Aronson, Inc., 1991, page 457-458

[2] Dr. Frank Eiklor, *A Time for Trumpets – not Piccolos!*, Orange, CA: Promise Publishing Co., 1988, page 93

had come into power, if the people had gotten out of their own little worlds and stood up against him, he would not have gotten away with what he did. Millions of people would not have died.

The Nazis even tested what they could get away with by instigating an anti-Jewish persecution called "*Kristallnacht*."[3] Many historians describe this terrible night and following day as the litmus test for Hitler. The world's reaction was tepid and the Nazis grew bolder in their anti-Jewish methodology until it soon led to the "*Shoah*."[4] Jewish homes were ransacked, as were shops, towns and villages, as SA stormtroopers and civilians destroyed buildings with sledgehammers, leaving the streets covered in pieces of smashed windows—the origin of the name "Night of Broken Glass." Ninety-one Jews were killed, and 30,000 Jewish men—a quarter of all Jewish men in Germany—were taken to concentration camps, where they were tortured for months, with over 1,000 of them dying. Around 1,668 synagogues were ransacked, and 267 set on fire. In Vienna

---

[3] *Kristallnacht*, also to referred to as the *Night of Broken Glass*, and also Reichskristallnacht, Pogromnacht, and Novemberpogrome, was a pogrom or series of attacks against Jews throughout Nazi Germany and parts of Austria on November 9–10, 1938.
[4] *Shoah*—a Hebrew word connoting catastrophe

alone 95 synagogues or houses of prayer were destroyed.

Kristallnacht was followed by further economic and political persecution of Jews, and is viewed by historians as part of Nazi Germany's broader racial policy, and the beginning of the Final Solution and the Holocaust.

Very few Germans complained. Granted, there were those individual cases of Christians, and other people, who cared. There were the ten Boom and Bonhoeffer families and the people in various resistance groups in the occupied lands. However, apart from the few who did care, most churches worldwide remained silent while millions of Jews and others (including other believers in Jesus) were shipped off to concentration camps to be put to death.

They remained silent as ships carrying escaping Jews were refused entry in one country after another, including the United States, until they had nowhere else to go but back to Hitler's ovens. Case in point – the S.S. St. Louis:

> On May 13 1939 the SS St. Louis set sail from Hamburg for Havana. On board were 937 Jewish refugees

fleeing persecution from Nazi Germany after the horror of Kristallnacht, the pogrom of shop-burning and mass arrests the previous November. Each passenger carried a valid visa for temporary entry into Cuba. It was one of the last ships to leave Nazi Germany before Europe was engulfed in war. As the boat approached Havana, the Cuban government declared the visas invalid and refused entry to the passengers. Subsequent negotiations with the Cuban government to permit the landing ended in failure. Similar attempts to seek entry to the United States also brought no respite. The United States, as the St. Louis steamed along its southern coast, refused to let the ship dock, in keeping with its straitjacket of a refugee policy, which would only tighten as the war progressed. After waiting 12 days in the port of Havana and off the Miami coast, the boat was forced to return to Europe.[5]

If Christians in Germany and the occupied lands had rallied to action as those in Norway did, Hitler would not have been successful in destroying so many people. In his book, *The HOLOCAUST, The Fate of European Jewry*, Leni Yahil writes:

> Other than the activists in the Norwegian underground, church people also came to the defense of the Jews. Many members of the Lutheran Church of Norway, the official state religion, as well as of other Protestant sects, had long resisted Quisling's [Vidkun Quisling, the governmental leader of Norway who gave in to Nazi pressure to persecute the Jews] government, and for months an appreciable number of clergy had been refusing to accept their salaries from the government as an expression of their opposition to the regime. On November 11 the Lutheran bishops in cooperation with clergy from several

---

[5] Copyright © 1999 Anthony Blechner, http://www.blechner.com/ssstlouis/

other Protestant sects sent a letter of protest to Quisling; in December it was twice read from the pulpit and was published as the New Year's message for 1943. After noting the arrest of all the Jewish males over the age of fifteen and the order confiscating Jewish property, the protest stated:

"For 91 years Jews have had a legal right to reside and to earn a livelihood in our country. Now they are being deprived of their property without warning...Jews have not been charged with transgression of the country's laws much less convicted of such transgressions by judicial procedure. Nevertheless, they are being punished as severely as the worst criminals are punished.

"They are being punished because of their racial background wholly and solely because they are Jews...Thus according to God's Word, all people have, in the first instance, the same human worth and thereby the same human rights. Our state authorities are by law obligated to respect this basic view...To remain silent about this legalized injustice against the Jews, would render ourselves co-guilty in this injustice."

This proclamation not only was circulated in Norway and Sweden but was read over Norwegian-language and other broadcasts of the BBC.[6]

There was, to their credit, one other people who stood united against the Nazi regime and said a resounding, "No!" to the exportation of Jews from their lands into the Nazi ovens.

The Danish people became the sole example of an entire nation rising as one to protect its citizens. While millions of people perished in Europe under Hitler's dictatorship, more than 90 percent of Denmark's Jews were saved because the people protected them.

When Jews were required to wear the yellow Star of David, identifying them to the Nazis as Jews, every person from King Christian X down to the

---

[6] Leni Yahil, *The HOLOCAUST, The Fate of European Jewry*, New York: Oxford University Press, 1990, page 396

butcher on the corner wore the star. Jews were taken into the homes of Christians and hidden in attics and cellars. Jewish property was maintained until after the war, when the rightful owners could reclaim it and renew their lives.

The king, when asked by the Nazis about the "Jewish question" replied, "There is no Jewish question in this country. There are only my people."[7] He risked his very life to defend his people; he was held a prisoner within his own country. Yet isn't that a small price for standing up for righteousness and justice and doing the right thing?

We, as believers, need to learn to think the same way. There is no *we* and *them*, but only us. "No man is an island,"[8] John Donne wrote. What happens to one affects the whole. When one group gets persecuted it affects us all.

We may not recognize its effect until later, but it will one day catch up to us. We cannot afford to be complacent and sit in our pews while others are suffering. We need to become activists like the

---

[7] Eiklor, *A Time for Trumpets*, page 93-94
[8] John Donne, *Devotions Upon Emergent Occasions*, No. 17 (1624)

Danes and stand up against oppression no matter where it takes place or how powerful the source.

On the other side of the spectrum, if you are a part of the group who is perpetrating this lie of anti-Semitism, then consider the fact that ruthless dictators such as Stalin and Hitler used people until they outlived their usefulness. Once people reached that stage, the dictators eliminated them (in one way or another).

Thin about Stalin with Lenin or Trotsky, or Hitler with the S.A. "Brownshirts." How valuable (or expendable) are you? Do you think that by maintaining a low profile that you will remain safe? Even if you remain "safe" in this world, do you think that you won't be held accountable for your "safe" silence while others suffered?

Every one of us will one day be held accountable for what we do in this life. Revelation 20:11-13 speaks of the Great White Throne judgment when the Lord will judge people according to their deeds. If your deeds do not stand in line with the Word of God, you will be forever condemned to the lake of fire.

It is not only on the basis of our deeds that judgment occurs. Even our words will condemn or justify us, according to Jesus in Matthew 12:36-37. In fact, it is not only by words that were said in a moment of emotion that we regret, but also words that we should have said, but didn't.

Did you walk on by when someone was badmouthing another race, remaining silent for fear of receiving the same? When someone was hurting another, did you slink away without getting involved? God knows and will hold you accountable.

What if you suspect that something is happening, but aren't willing to find out for sure and take action against it? Are you an ostrich which prefers to bury its head beneath the sand when trouble comes?

The stench of death would often pervade and hover over the villages near the death camps of Poland and Germany, yet the people either out of fear or out of a lack of caring remained silent as millions perished. They preferred instead to remain officially ignorant of the occurrences at the death camps in their neighborhood. In the law and in God's justice, ignorance is no excuse. We are all accountable for what we are able to do or say – no matter what the cost.

The Bible clearly speaks of a resurrection of the righteous and the unrighteous. The righteous progress to eternal life and the unrighteous go to eternal contempt (Daniel 12:2). Which eternal do you choose: life or contempt? Is eternal contempt worth the life you are living now? Why not repent, ask God for forgiveness, and live righteously?

Are you willing to jeopardize some of the blessings on the other side (the infinite side) for the relative comfort and security of this side (the finite side)?

Now is the opportunity you have in this brief life. After you die, it is too late.

Stand now for what is righteous and true in this life so you will have a rewarded eternal life in the resurrection to come...

Chapter Two

The Plot

As I stated in the first chapter, a lie *always* has a motivation behind it. There are no accidental lies. Therefore, what could possibly be the motivation behind the lies against the Jewish people – a motivation so secret that even the perpetrators themselves are unaware of it?

In order to uncover this motivation, we need to go to the first book of the Bible: Genesis. In chapter 3, after the man and woman had sinned against God and partook of the forbidden fruit, God promised them an ultimate redeemer.

This redeemer would be born of the seed of a woman and would crush the Adversary on the head (verse 15). We can tell that Eve thought the redeemer would be Cain, her firstborn (4:1) when she said, "I have gotten a man-child...the Lord." Although many translations insert the words, "with the help of" those words do not appear in the original Hebrew Scripture. So in other words, Eve thought Cain was the man-child spoken of in

Genesis 3:15 who would redeem them from their sins. As we know, he wasn't. God had someone else in mind and He would progressively reveal the identity of this redeemer in time.

He would be a descendant of Abraham. God promised to give Abraham a specific land, to make of him a great nation (Genesis 12:1-3) and to make him a way for all the nations to be blessed.

This redeemer would be a descendant of Isaac (Genesis 26:3-5) and of Jacob (Genesis 28:13-15), who were blessed by God with the same promises given to Abraham. Furthermore, the promise that "a star shall come forth from Jacob" given in Numbers 24:17 pointed toward the redeemer as a descendant of Jacob and none other.

Messianic prophecy upon messianic prophecy in the Hebrew Scriptures were given so it would be clear that the "Messiah" (Annointed One" would come only through the Hebrew people and according to Genesis 49:10 specifically through Judah (the tribe by which the Jewish people are named).

With this in mind, who would stand to lose the most if this redeemer of mankind came on the scene? Why, the one whose head was to be crushed, of course (Genesis 3:15). So if God was willing to identify the very group of people from whom this redeemer would spring, then Satan would be accommodating enough to see to it that this group of people would be destroyed, if at all possible.

Thus, he tried to destroy them in Egypt by killing the Hebrew male children (Exodus 1-2). He tried to destroy them in the Wilderness (Exodus 17:8-13). He tried to destroy them in Persia (Book of Esther). He tried to assimilate them (and thus prevent the Messiah) through Antiochus Epiphanies (Book of Maccabees).

Finally, when it was clear that the Messiah was already born as announced by the Magi (Matthew 2), he tried to kill the Messiah through King Herod. Herod had the children in Bethlehem and its environs killed.

In failing to kill the Messiah as a child, he played into God's hand and orchestrated His crucifixion. In placing Jesus on the cross, he bruised His heel; but incurred a blow to his head by the resurrection of Jesus from the dead. Thus the prophecy in Genesis was fulfilled.

So what is the motive of the lie behind anti-Semitism? Destroy the Jewish people and you destroy the Redeemer.

Oh, the perpetrators of the lie thought they were acting with noble intent; yet they were deceived by the greatest liar of all. "Noble causes" were the smoke screen that hid the true motive for the destruction of the Jewish people.

The Nazis thought the world would thank them after they had "purified" it by disposing of the Jewish people. They thought they were acting with the noblest of motives in defending the white Aryan race.

In reality, they, like the perpetrators against the Jewish people throughout were pawns of the greatest deceiver of all: Satan. He is the adversary of not just the Jewish people, but of all mankind, for man is made in the image of Almighty God, whom he really hates.

Logic says that since the Redeemer who won the battle has already come, and fulfilled His earthly mission, Satan would just leave the Jewish people alone. After all, their job was finished when they gave birth to the Messiah. The Messiah isn't to return to this earth again through the Jewish people, is He? He is to return again in power and glory from the skies (Revelation 19).

So, why is Satan still persecuting the Jewish people? There are two reasons: First, he hates them (Revelation 12) and Second, Jesus' return is dependent upon the Jewish people saying, "Blessed is He who comes in the name of the Lord" (Matthew 23:37-39 NAS).

We who believe in Jesus recognize Him as the Incarnate Word of God. Since God's Word is always true, then Jesus' words will also be true. Now, as Jesus looked upon the Temple from the Mount of Olives, He spoke certain words to her alone that must ring true also. It is important to realize that He was *not* speaking to Christians here, but Jews.

Therefore, it will not be Christians who call Jesus back, but Jews! If the Christians were able to call Him back, we would have done it long, long ago. It is the Jewish people, particularly the Jewish leaders in Jerusalem, who hold the power to call Him back by uttering these words. We are speaking of a future event that is still awaiting fulfillment! Jerusalem must still say these words, or the word of Jesus is not true!

If Jesus were wrong in these words to Jerusalem, He could be just as wrong when He says, "I am the way, the truth, and the life; no one comes to the Father, but through Me." (John 14:6 NAS) If God's Word is wrong in just one place relative to one thing, His Word also could be wrong relative to our salvation and then our salvation would be in jeopardy. Thus, it is a good thing that God's Word is correct in every little detail.

It is a fact that Satan knows God's Word and tries to thwart God's purposes. That is why Satan still wants to destroy the Jewish people. He reasons: No Jewish people means no-one to call the Messiah. If there is no return of the Messiah, then there is no final defeat. Satan's conclusion is absolutely correct, for it is in Jesus' return that he finds his final defeat (Revelation 20).

Just how does Satan work to destroy God's plan? He works through people, many who, from their own perspective, are well meaning. Pharaoh thought he was protecting his own people (Exodus 1:8-10), and so did Adolf Hitler. But both were dead wrong, intentions notwithstanding, because they stood in opposition to God with respect to God's people.

It is understandable that leaders of nations desire to protect their national interests, yet there is a superseding interest that must be placed above that of the nation and individual. It is God's interest. What God wants should be paramount and it behooves the nation and the individual to do what God wants.

When God said to Abram, "I will bless those who bless you, and I will curse him who curses you" (Genesis 12:3a NKJ), it behooves the nation and the individual to bless Abraham through his descendants. Any nation or individual who stands in opposition to this divinely ordained statement stands to lose all, and will invoke God's curse.

Every nation throughout history that cursed Israel has died accursed. Yet Israel still exists in spite of the attempts to cause its demise. God attests to this continuing existence in Jeremiah 31:35-37: If the order of the moon and the stars and the sea cease, then Israel will cease. End of story. It is as simple as that.

This means that only One can make this promise: One who is greater than the moon, sun, stars, and sea. It is He who controls all these things and He who causes Israel to exist. The greatest attestation to the existence of God is the continued existence of the Jewish people throughout time. If Satan could kill all the Jews, then God's Word is not true...for He would not be able to keep this promise. God, then would be a liar and His promises not able to be kept. This is a scary thought, for that would mean that we, who are believers in Jesus, really might not actually be saved.

It is unfortunate that most of the perpetrators of the lies against the Jewish people are ignorant of what is truly happening. Perhaps if they were aware of the true motivation and its consequences they would not be party to such a plot. It is understandable that if they were not believers in God or God's Word, they would not be aware of a plot at all.

What is truly sad is that Satan doesn't just recruit unbelievers to do his dirty work. Much of the destruction pointed at the Jewish people has come from the hands of those who professed to be Christian, who supposedly know God's Word. Many of Satan's biggest pawns are found within the Church herself. The Body of the Jewish Messiah is perhaps the greatest destroyer of the

Messiah's people: the Jewish people and the true believers from all nations who are grafted into her.

Chapter Three

The Perpetration of the Lie in the Church

Shortly after Peter's "Good Confession" in Matthew 16:13-19, Jesus began to show His disciples that "He must go to Jerusalem and suffer many things from the elders and chief priests and scribes, and be killed, and be raised up on the third day" (Matthew 16:21 NAS). Upon hearing this, Peter took the Lord aside and began to rebuke Him, saying, "God forbid it, Lord! This shall never happen to You" (verse 22 NAS). But Jesus turned and said to Peter, "Get behind Me, Satan! You are a stumbling block to Me; for you are not setting your mind on God's interests, but man's" (verse 23 NAS).

At that moment, Peter, a good man and a cherished disciple of the Lord, was being used of Satan. Although his intent was good – he did not want to see his Master killed – the purpose behind the intent was evil. If Satan could have thwarted God's purposes by keeping Jesus from the cross, then mankind would still be lost in sin. [It was Satan's desire to kill Jesus, preferably outside of what the Scripture said – so that God's Word could be made void. For instance, Jesus could have died by stoning (John 8:59) or in the Garden, when He sweated drops of blood (Matthew 27:26) or while He was carrying the cross in His weakened state (Matthew 27:32). Though Satan, as alluded to earlier, orchestrated Jesus' death on the cross, he would rather have had Him die off the cross to invalidate God's Word.]

In any event, what is interesting about the Matthew 16:13-19 passage is that it shows Satan does not simply use evil people to propagate his purposes; he often uses the very people of God to do his dastardly deeds.

Now, I do not purport to know the intent of the hearts of the people I quote in this chapter. I am not God. Nevertheless, I can see that these people in the Church, whether through understanding or ignorance, have bought into and propagated a lie initiated from the pit of Hell, a lie against the people whom God calls, "Chosen."

It is important for us to realize that not everyone in the Kingdom of Heaven is a believer in God. Matthew 12:47-50 describes the Kingdom of Heaven as a dragnet cast into the sea and gathering fish of every kind. There are good fist and there are bad fish. It says that at the end of the age the good and the bad fish will be separated and that the bad will be cast into the furnace of fire.

I believe that some of these men that I quote in this chapter were bad fish who had a great deal of influence over the Church, deceiving people into believing that their teachings were of God. Ultimately, the bad fish will be judged and cast into the fires of Hell. Others, I believe, are like Peter, who with good intent acted and spoke out of ignorance. Which is which, I shall leave up to God. It is He who shall separate the good from the bad at the end of the age.

It is not our job to judge the man. Nevertheless, it is up to us to recognize and reject the lie spoken through the man's lips and to stand up against it in the Body of Messiah.

That is what Jesus did with Peter and that is what we are obligated to do as people of God, who are followers of "the Way, and the Truth, and the Life (John 14:6 AMP).

Most Christians today are unaware of the anti-Semitic teachings of these men and how those teachings have influenced Christian thinking even to this very day. That is the only reason I am placing their quotes within this book.

I believe that it is imperative for us to recognize that their influence is still within the Church and that we must speak out against such teachings whenever they surface in our congregations and Christian circles.

Now, in all fairness to the denominations these men belonged to or founded, most have repudiated these men's teachings of anti-Semitism. The Lutherans have renounced Luther's anti-Semitic diatribes and the Catholics have renounced anti-Semitism in Vatican II. Yet, in spite of the renunciation of these teachings, many within Christian circles still hold anti-Semitic attitudes fostered by Church teachings, especially those who hold to "White Supremist" or "Aryan" doctrines.

Origen (185-254 A.D.)

According to Hal Lindsey in his book, The Road to Holocaust:

> The man most responsible for changing the way the Church interpreted prophecy was Origen. He was a leading teacher of theology and philosophy at the influential catechetical school of Alexandria, Egypt at the beginning of the third century. Church historian A.H. Newman reports, "Origen was the first to reduce the allegorical method of interpretation to a system...His method of Scripture interpretation was soon adopted throughout the church, and prevailed throughout the Middle Ages. In this particular Origen's influence was bad, and only bad." It must be noted that Origen was not an evil man. In fact, he was a scholarly Christian philosopher with a courageous faith who lived a humble and ascetic life. But because of his

desire to harmonize the New Testament with the philosophy of Plato, he powerfully introduced, taught, and spread the allegorical method of interpreting the Scriptures, particularly in the area of prophecy. From this seemingly harmless fact of Church history evolved a system of prophetic interpretation that created the atmosphere in which Christian anti-Semitism took root and spread. Using this method of prophetic interpretation, church theologians began to develop the idea that the Israelites had permanently forfeited all their covenants by rejecting Jesus as the Messiah. This view taught that these covenants now belong to the Church, and that it is the only true Israel now and forever. The view also taught that the Jews will never again have a future as a Divinely chosen people, and that the Messiah will never establish His Messianic

Kingdom on earth that was promised to them.[9]

"For some of his doctrines," wrote Daniel Gruber in his book, *The Church and the Jews, the Biblical Relationship*, "Origen was considered by many to be a heretic. During his lifetime, he was excommunicated by two church councils held in Alexandria in 231 and 232 AD. After his death as well, his views were officially condemned by some in the Church as heretical. Today there is no question that some of his teachings could be considered heretical enough to place him outside the believing Church.

"Nevertheless, most of the Greek fathers of the third and fourth centuries stood more or less under the influence of the spirit and the works of Origen, without adopting all his peculiar speculative views. The most distinguished among his disciples are Gregory Thaumaturgus, Dionysus of Alexandria, surnamed the Great, Heraclas, Hieracas, Pamphilus; in a wider sense also Eusebius, Gregory of Nyssa and other eminent divines of the Nicene age.

---

[9] Hal Lindsey, *The Road to Holocaust*, New York, New York: Bantam Books, 1989, pages 7-8

"Though these men of the third and fourth century church did not accept all the teachings which Origen's system of interpretation generated, they did accept the system itself: With only the sparse historical information that we have available, we are still able to trace the transmission of that system. It is Origen's system of interpretation that produces the anti-Judaic 'New Israel' theology where the Church replaces the Jews in the plan and purpose of God."[10]

Constantine the Great (280-337 A.D.)

> We wish to make it known to the Jews and their elders and their patriarchs that if, after the enactment of this law, any one of them dares to attack with stones or some other manifestation of anger another who has fled their dangerous sect and attached himself to the worship of God [Christianity], he must speedily be given to the flames and burn~ together with all his accomplices.

---

[10] Daniel Gruber, *The Church and the Jews, The Biblical Relationship*, Springfield, MO: General Council of the Assemblies of God, 1991, page 12

Moreover, if any one of the population should join their abominable sect and attend their meetings, he will bear with them the deserved penalties.[11]

Saint Gregory of Nyssa (335-394 A.D.)

Slayers of the Lord, murderers of the prophets, enemies of God, haters of God, adversaries of grace, enemies of their fathers' faith, advocates of the devil, brood of vipers, slanderers, scoffers, men of darkened minds, leaven of the Pharisees, congregation of demons, sinners, wicked men, stoners, and haters of goodness.[12]

Saint John Chrysostom (344-407 A.D.)

What is this disease? The festivals of the pitiful and miserable Jews are

---

[11] Jacob R. Marcus, *The Jew in the Medieval World*, New York: Atheneum, 1973, page 4

[12] St. Gregory of Nyssa, *Homilies on the Resurrection*, 5; as quoted in Gould, *What Did They Think*, 24

soon to march upon us one after the other and in quick succession: the feast of Trumpets, the feast of Tabernacles, the fasts. There are many in our ranks who say they think as we do. Yet some of these are going to watch the festivals and others will join the Jews in keeping their feasts and observing their fasts. I wish to drive this perverse custom from the Church right now. My homilies against the Anomoeans can be put off to another time, and the postponement would cause no harm. But now that the Jewish festivals are close by and at the very door, if I should fail to cure those who are sick with the Judaizing disease. I am afraid that, because of their ill-suited association and deep ignorance, some Christians may partake in the Jews' transgressions; once they have done so, I fear my homilies on these transgressions will be in vain. For if they hear no word from me today, they will then join the Jews in their fasts; once they have committed this sin it will be useless for me to apply the remedy.[13]

Many, I know, respect the Jews and think that their present way of life is a venerable one. This is why I hasten to uproot and tear out this deadly opinion. I said that the synagogue is no better than a theater and I bring forward a prophet as my witness. Surely the Jews are not more deserving of belief than their prophets. "You had a harlot's brow; you became shameless before all". Where a harlot has set herself up, that place is a brothel. But the synagogue is not only a brothel and a theater; it also is a den of robbers and a lodging for wild beasts. Jeremiah said: "Your house has become for me the den of a hyena". He does not simply say "of wild beast", but "of a filthy wild beast", and again: "I have abandoned my house, I have cast off my inheritance". But when God forsakes a people, what hope of salvation is

---

[13] St. John Chrysostom, Homilies Against the Jews, Homily 1:5

left? When God forsakes a place, that place becomes the dwelling of demons.[14]

Our churches are not like that; they are truly frightening and filled with fear. God's presence makes a place frightening because he has power over life and death. In our churches we hear countless homilies on eternal punishments, on rivers of fire, on the venomous worm, on bonds that cannot be burst, or exterior darkness. But the Jews neither know nor dream of these things. They live for their bellies, they gape for the things of this world, their condition is not better than that of pigs or goats because of their wanton ways and excessive gluttony. They know but one thing: to fill their bellies and be drunk, to get all cut and bruised, to be hurt and wounded while fighting for their favorite charioteers.[15]

---

[14] Ibid., Homily 3:1
[15] Ibid., Homily 4:1

Since there are some who think of the synagogue as a holy place, I must say a few words to them. Why do you reverence that place? Must you not despise it, hold it in abomination, run away from it? They answer that the Law and the books of the prophets are kept there. What is this? Will any place where these books are be a holy place? By no means! This is the reason above all others why I hate the synagogue and abhor it. They have the prophets but not believe them; they read the sacred writings but reject their witness-and this is a mark of men guilty of the greatest outrage.[16]

Saint Augustine (354-430 A.D.)

He did many miracles that He might commend God in Himself, some of which, even as many as seemed sufficient to proclaim Him, are contained in the evangelic Scripture. The first of these is, that He was so

[16] Ibid., Homily 5:2

wonderfully born, and the last, that with His body raised up again from the dead He ascended into heaven. But the Jews who slew Him, and would not believe in Him, because it behooved Him to die and rise again, were yet more miserably wasted by the Romans, and utterly rooted out from their kingdom, where aliens had already ruled over them, and were dispersed through the lands (so that indeed there is no place where they are not), and are thus by their own Scriptures a testimony to us that we have not forged the prophecies about Christ. And very many of them, considering this, even before His passion, but chiefly after His resurrection, believed on Him, of whom it was predicted, "Though the number of the children of Israel be as the sand of the sea, the remnant shall be saved." But the rest are blinded, of whom it was predicted, "Let their table be made before them a trap, and a retribution, and a stumbling-block. Let their eyes be darkened lest they

see, and bow down their back alway."
Therefore, when they do not believe
our Scriptures, their own, which they
blindly read, are fulfilled in them, lest
perchance any one should say that the
Christians have forged these
prophecies about Christ which are
quoted under the name of the sibyl, or
of others, if such there be, who do not
belong to the Jewish people. For us,
indeed, those suffice which are quoted
from the books of our enemies, to
whom we make our acknowledgment,
on account of this testimony which, in
spite of themselves, they contribute
by their possession of these books,
while they themselves are dispersed
among all nations, wherever the
Church of Christ is spread abroad. For
a prophecy about this thing was sent
before in the Psalms, which they also
read, where it is written, "My God,
His mercy shall prevent me. My God
hath shown me concerning mine
enemies, that Thou shalt not slay
them, lest they should at last forget
Thy law: disperse them in Thy

might." Therefore God has shown the Church in her enemies the Jews the grace of His compassion, since, as saith the apostle, "their offence is the salvation of the Gentiles." And therefore He has not slain them, that is, He has not let the knowledge that they are Jews be lost in them, although they have been conquered by the Romans, lest they should forget the law of God, and their testimony should be of no avail in this matter of which we treat. But it was not enough that he should say, "Slay them not, lest they should at last forget Thy law," unless he had also added, "Disperse them;" because if they had only been in their own land with that testimony of the Scriptures, and not everywhere, certainly the Church which is everywhere could not have had them as witnesses among all nations to the prophecies which were sent before concerning Christ.[17]

---

[17] Augustine, *The City of God*, as Translated by Marcus Dods, Book XVIII, Chapter 46

Saint Jerome (374-419 A.D.)

In his The Jews in the Roman Empire (*Les Juifs dan L'Empire Romain*) he wrote: "The Jews seek nothing but to have children, possess riches and be healthy. They seek all earthly things, but think nothing of heavenly things; for this reason they are mercenaries."[18]

Saint Fulgentius of Ruspe (467-533 A.D.)

Most firmly hold and never doubt that not only pagans, but also Jews, all heretics, and all schismatics who finish this life outside of the Catholic Church, will go into eternal fire prepared for the devil and his angels.[19]

Pope Pious IV (1499-1565 A.D.)

We order that each and every Jew of both sexes in Our Temporal Dominions and in all the cities, lands,

---

[18] Jerome, *Les Juifs dan L'Empire Romain*, volume 2 (Paris: Guenthne, 1914), as quoted in Gould, *What Did They Think*, 27-28
[19] *Writings* (510 A.D.) as quoted in Gould, *What Did They Think*, 28

places, and baronies subject to them, shall depart completely out of the confines thereof within the space of three months and after these letters shall have been made public.[20]

Martin Luther (1483-1546 A.D.)

What then shall we Christians do with this damned, rejected race of Jews? Since they live among us and we know about their lying and blasphemy and cursing, we cannot tolerate them if we do not wish to share in their lies, curses, and blasphemy. In this way we cannot quench the inextinguishable fire of divine rage nor convert the Jews. We must prayerfully and reverentially practice a merciful severity. Perhaps we may save a few from the fire and flames [of hell]. We must not seek vengeance. They are surely being punished a thousand times more than we might wish them. Let me give you my honest advice.

---

[20] Gould, *What Did They Think*, 54

First, their synagogues should be set on fire, and whatever does not burn up should be covered or spread over with dirt so that no one may ever be able to see a cinder or stone of it. And this ought to be done for the honor of God and of Christianity in order that God may see that we are Christians, and that we have not wittingly tolerated or approved of such public lying, cursing, and blaspheming of His Son and His Christians.

Secondly, their homes should likewise be broken down and destroyed. For they perpetrate the same things there that they do in their synagogues. For this reason they ought to be put under one roof or in a stable, like gypsies, in order that they may realize that they are not masters in our land, as they boast, but miserable captives, as they complain of incessantly before God with bitter wailing.

Thirdly, they should be deprived of their prayer-books and Talmuds in which such idolatry, lies, cursing, and blasphemy are taught.

Fourthly, their rabbis must be forbidden under threat of death to teach any more...

Fifthly, passport and traveling privileges should be absolutely forbidden to the Jews. For they have no business in the rural districts since they are not nobles, nor officials, nor merchants, nor the like. Let them stay at home...If you princes and nobles do not close the road legally to such exploiters, then some troop ought to ride against them, for they will learn from this pamphlet what the Jews are and how to handle them and that they ought not to be protected. You ought not, you cannot protect them, unless in the eyes of God you want to share all their abomination...

To sum up, dear princes and nobles who have Jews in your domains, if this advice of mine does not suit you, then find a better one so that you and we may all be free of this insufferable devilish burden - the Jews...[21]

In 1924 at a Christian gathering in Berlin, Adolf Hitler, a professed Christian, stood before thousands of Christians, and with a standing ovation said:

"I believe that today I am acting in accordance with the will of Almighty God. As I announce the most important work that Christians could undertake and that is to be against the Jews and get rid of them once and for all. We are doing the work of the Lord and let's get on with it." Hitler stated, "Martin Luther has been the greatest encouragement of my life. Luther was a great man. He was a giant. Within one blow he heralded the coming of the new dawn and the new age. He saw clearly that the Jews need to be destroyed and we're only beginning to see that we need to carry this work on." Hitler followed to the letter,

---

[21] Martin Luther, *Concerning the Jews and Their Lies* (1543); as quoted in Jacob R. Marcus, *The Jew in the Medieval World* (New York: Atheneum, 1973) 167-169

Luther's treatise on how to exterminate the Jews. Martin Luther preached his last sermon avidly against the Jews and died four days later. Indeed, Nazi leader Streicher at his Nuremberg trial stated, "I have never said anything that Martin Luther did not say."[22]

In his book, *The Road to Holocaust*, Hal Lindsey notes:

The *Encyclopedia Judaica* rightly comments about Luther's tract; "Short of the Auschwitz oven and extermination, the whole Nazi Holocaust is pre-outlined here." Is it any wonder that Hitler and Julius Streicher quoted Martin Luther as justification for their murderous "Final Solution for the Jews?[23]

We could go on and on through the centuries of "Christian" diatribe against the Jewish people. This sort of theological garbage should sicken those who are believers in Jesus.

---

[22] http://www.diaspora-scrapbook.org/Antisemitism.aspx
[23] Lindsey, *The Road to Holocaust*, 24

Sadly, the warning of the apostle Paul in Romans 11:18 has largely gone unheeded by these Christian men. "Do not be arrogant toward the branches; but if you are arrogant, remember that it is not you who supports the root, but the root supports you."

The arrogance of these gentile Christians who are "unnaturally grafted in" to the root (Israel) toward the natural branches (the Jewish people) can easily be seen in their words. They should fear as Paul says and not be arrogant, for God can just as easily break them off. God still loves His people (Romans 11:1-2) and will save them after all the Gentiles who will be saved come into the root (Romans 11:25-26). Arrogance such as we have seen does not belong to the Church!

Anti-Semitic Canonical Laws

Church law throughout the ages has also been extremely anti-Semitic, thus paralleling the anti-Jewish measures taken in the Nazi era. For the sake of easily showing both, I have included a table taken from Raoul Hilberg in his book, *The Destruction of the European Jews* (Reprinted by

Permission of the publisher, Jason Aronson, Inc., Northvale, NJ):[24]

Canonical Law and Anti-Jewish Measures

Canonical Law	Nazi Measure
Prohibition of intermarriage and of sexual intercourse between Christians and Jews, Synod of Elvira, 306	Law for the Protection of German Blood and Honor, September 15, 1935 (RGB1 I, 1146)
Jews and Christians not permitted to eat together, Synod of Elvira, 306	Jews barred from dining cars (Transport Minister to Interior Minister, December 30, 1939, Document NG-3995)
Jews not allowed to hold public office, Synod of Clermont, 535	Laws for the Re-establishment of the Professional Civil Service, April 7, 1933 (RGB1 I, 175)
Jews not allowed to employ Christian servants or possess Christian slaves, 3rd Synod of Orleans, 538	Law for the Protection of German Blood and Honor, September 15, 1935

---

[24] Raoul Hilberg, *The Destruction of the European Jews*, New York: Holmes & Meier, 1985, as quoted in Gould, *What Did They Think*, 381-382

Jews not permitted to show themselves in the streets during Passion Week, 3rd Synod of Orleans, 538	Decree authorizing local authorities to bar Jews from the streets on certain days (i.e. Nazi holidays, December 3, 1938 (RGB1 I, 1676)
Burning of Talmud and other books, 12th Synod of Toledo, 681	Book burnings in Nazi Germany
Christians not permitted to patronize Jewish doctors, Trulanic Synod, 692	Decree of July 25, 1938 (RGB 1 I, 969)
Christians not permitted in Jewish homes, Synod of Narbonne, 1050	Directive by Goering providing for concentration of Jews in houses, December 28, 1938 (Borman to Rosenberg, January 17, 1939, PS-69)
Jews obliged to pay taxes for support of the Church to the same extent as Christians, Synod of Gerona, 1078	The "Sozialausgleichsabgabe" which provided that the Jews pay a special income tax in lieu of donations for Party purposes imposed on Nazis, December 24, 1940 (RGB 1 I, 1666)
Prohibition of Sunday work,	

Synod of Szabolcs, 1092	
Jews not permitted to be plaintiffs, or witnesses against Christians in the Courts, 3rd Lateran Council, 1179, Canon 26	Proposal by the Party Chancellery that Jews not be permitted to institute civil suits. September 9, 1942 (Bormann to Justice Ministry, September 9, 1942, NG-151)
Jews not permitted to withhold inheritance from descendants who had accepted Christianity, 3rd Lateran Council, 1179, Canon 26	Decree empowering the Justice Ministry to void the wills offending the "sound judgment of the people" July 31, 1938 (RGB 1, I, 937)
The marking of Jewish clothes with a badge, 4th Lateran Council, 1215, Canon 68 (Copied from the legislation by Caliph Omar II (634-44), who had decreed that Christians wear blue belts and Jews, yellow belts)	Decree of September 1, 1941 (RGB 1 I,547)
Construction of new synagogues	Destruction of synagogues in entire Reich, November 10,

prohibited, Council of Oxford, 1222	1938 (Heydrich to Goering November 11, 1938, PS-3058)
Christians not permitted to attend Jewish ceremonies, Synod of Vienna, 1267	Friendly relations with Jews prohibited, October 24, 1941 (Gestapo directive, L-15)
Jews not permitted to dispute with simple Christian people about the tenets of the Catholic religion, Synod of Vienna, 1267	
Compulsory ghettos, Synod of Breslau, 1267	Order by Heydrich, September 21, 1939 (PS-3363)
Christians not permitted to sell or rent real estate to Jews, Synod of Ofen, 1279	Decree providing for compulsory sale of Jewish real estate, December 3, 1938 (RGB 1 I, 1709)
Adoption by a Christian of the Jewish religion or return by a baptized Jew to the Jewish religion defined as a heresy, Synod of	Adoption by a Christian of the Jewish religion places him in jeopardy of being treated as a Jew. Decision by Oberlandesgericht Konigsberg, 4th Zivilsenat, June 26, 1942 (Die

Mainz, 1310	Judenfrage [Vertrauliche Beilagte], November 1, 1942, pp. 82-83)
Sale or transfer of Church articles to Jews prohibited, Synod of Lavour, 1368	
Jews not permitted to act as agents in the conclusion of contracts between Christians, especially marriage contracts, Council of Basel, 1434, Sessio XIX	Decree of July 6, 1938, providing liquidation of Jewish real estate agent brokerage agencies and marriage age catering to non-Jews (RGB 1 I, 823)
Jews not permitted to obtain academic degrees, Council of Basel, 1434, Sessio XIX	Law against overcrowding of German schools and universities, April 25, 1933 (RGB 1 I, 225)

It is interesting to note the parallels between what the Church decreed and what the Nazis actually implemented. Hal Lindsey comments in his book, *The Road to Holocaust*,

> Raoul Hilberg makes some observations about this issue that all

should weigh carefully. Hilberg maintains that the Holocaust did not happen in a theological vacuum, but rather as the inevitable result of three consecutive anti-Jewish policies that occurred throughout Western history.

Hilberg says: "Anti-Jewish policies and anti-Jewish actions did not have their beginnings in 1933. For many centuries, and in many countries, the Jews have been victims of destructive action.

"What was the object of these activities? What were the aims of those who persisted in these anti-Jewish deeds? Throughout Western history, three consecutive policies have been applied against Jewry in its dispersion.

"To summarize: Since the fourth century after Christ, there have been three anti-Jewish policies: Conversion, expulsion, and annihilation. The second [expulsion] appeared as an alternative to the first, and the third [annihilation] as an alternative to the second.

"The Nazi destruction process did not come out of a void; it was the culmination of a cyclical trend. We have observed the trend in three successive goals of anti-Jewish administrators. 1) The missionaries of Christianity had said in effect: You have no right to live among us as Jews. 2) The secular rulers who followed had proclaimed: You have no right to live among us. 3) The German Nazis at last decreed: You have no right to live.

"These progressively more drastic goals brought in their wake a slow and steady growth of anti-Jewish actions and anti-Jewish thinking. The process began with the attempt to drive the Jews into Christianity. The development was continued in order to force the victims into exile. It was finished when the Jews were driven to their deaths.

"The German Nazis, then, did not discard the past; they built upon it. They did not begin the development; they completed it."[25]

What the theologians proposed in theory, the Nazis carried out in fact. No doubt Martin Luther did not envision a Holocaust ensuing from his words. It is doubtful that anyone could have imagined the outcome of the process of his words – and the words of other theologians – had set in motion. Yet, for all that, we cannot excuse their words with pleas of ignorance. The truth that opposed their anti-Semitic statements was staring them right in the face in the Scriptures.

The essence of the Gospel of Jesus is love for all mankind. Even if we have enemies, we are to love them according to Christ – not kill them or deprive them of their belongings, their freedom, their families, or their lives. What these men proposed ultimately smacked of exactly the opposite to the teachings of the Lord they claimed as their own. For that, they shall have to answer to God.

---

[25] Raoul Hilsberg, *The Destruction of the European Jews*, 1-4; as quoted in Lindsey, *The Road to Holocaust*, 6-7

As for us, we have the opportunity to learn lessons from their mistakes and correct the wrongs when we see them occur. We need to stand against anti-Semitism, especially when it comes under the guise of Christianity and when it rears its own ugly head, or we will share in these men's sins before God. We have it within our power to love instead of hate for that is the true essence of the Gospel of Christ.

Chapter Four

Persecutions against the Jewish People

Although most Christians are unaware of the various persecutions against the Jewish people, apart from the Holocaust, that is not the case with the Jewish people. They remember – and they remember well.

What is most tragic is they remember these persecutions as coming from "Christians" or from "Christian" nations. They are not without justification for thinking this way.

As Jews were killed by Nazis or Nazi sympathizers on Saturday, their survivors would see the Nazi murderers go to church on Sunday.

Also, with the Church stirring up such virulent anti-Semitic sentiment, this interpretation becomes very plausible.

This chapter looks back at history and summarizes the persecutions against the Jewish people over the millennia – when they occurred, why they were instigated (if known), and how many Jewish lives (if recorded) were lost as a result of these persecutions.

These persecutions take many forms; they can range from forcing the Jewish people to wear certain clothing all the way to mass murdering and destroying entire communities. Because there are so many persecutions, I will try not to embellish the events with too much detail. Rather, I will make a simple statement as to their chronology and the event. The point is: every believer should know the scope of the persecutions that have been carried out against the Jewish people, many in the Name of the very Messiah who loves them (Romans 11:28-29).

For full details of all persecutions against the Jewish people, I recommend, *The Jewish Time Line Encyclopedia* (compiled by Mattis Kantor, Jason Aronson, Inc., Northvale, NJ). Much of the following material is condensed from this book and is used by permission.

Since I am dealing with the overall persecution against the Hebrew people and not specifically those of Christian anti-Semitism, we will begin with the persecution in Egypt as related in the Bible:

1429 B.C., The enslavement in Egypt (see Bible – Exodus). Destruction of the Hebrew male children, an unknown number of male children killed.

362 B.C., Haman (see Bible – Esther) decreed destruction of Jewish people. Though no statistics are known, the Jewish people had to fight some who opposed them.

69. A.D., Over 1 million Jewish people died as a result of battle, hunger, and disease after a failed revolt against Rome. Almost 100,000 Jews were taken captive to Rome to fight wild animals in Roman coliseums.

133 A.D., 580,000 Jewish people were killed after the failed Bar Kochbah revolt.

414 A.D., First expulsion of Jews. Jews were expelled from Alexandra by Christian authorities.

535 A.D., Justinian I, emperor of the Byzantine Empire, ordered the closing of all synagogues. Ordered other repressive decreed against the Jews.

576 A.D., First forced-baptism. Five hundred Jews of Clermont Ferrand in France were forced to be baptized. Many Jews fled.

582 A.D., Frankish King Chilperic I forced many Jews to become Christians.

612 A.D., The Jews of Spain were ordered to convert or leave.

694 A.D., The Jews of Spain were accused of plotting to overthrow the Christian Visigoth government. This government had been continuously enacting laws to convert or expel them. Many Jews fled but many were forcibly converted.

722 A.D., Many Jews were forced to accept Christianity in the Byzantine Empire. Many left Constantinople and other parts of the Empire.

850 A.D., Jews of Iraq were required by their Muslim Arab rulers to wear a yellow patch.

931 A.D., The Jews in parts of Italy were forced to convert to Christianity. Many were massacred in Bari.

1007 A.D., Many Jews were killed throughout France and many were forced to convert to Christianity.

1096 A.D., First Crusade. Pope Urban II declared a Crusade to capture Jerusalem. Thousands of Jews were massacred by the masses along the way. A summary of massacres follows:

Jews of Bavaria; of Worms, Germany; of Prussia; of Mainz, Germany (1,000); of Bachrach, Germany; of Cologne, Germany; of Xanten, Germany; of Mehr, Germany; of Troyes and Metz, France; of Regensburg, Germany; of Prague, Hungary; and of Pressburg, Hungary were massacred. The dead numbered in the tens of thousands, and many were forced to be baptized.

1099 A.D., Jerusalem captured by Crusaders. They forced all the Jews into a synagogue which they then set on fire, killing almost all. As the synagogue burned, they marched around the burning building singing, "Christ, we adore Thee."

1125 A.D., Jews were expelled from Ghent and from the rest of the province of Flanders.

1144 A.D., First recorded blood libel took place in Norwich, England. Blood libel is a lie that says that the Jews use a Christian child's blood for ritual purposes in the Passover Seder. The Biblical prohibition in the Torah (Leviticus 17:10-14) against the ingesting of blood should be sufficient proof that Jews will not do this; nevertheless, many Christians through the ages have believed this lie and some to this day continue to believe it.

1147 A.D., The second group of Crusaders attacked Jewish communities in their path. Pope Eugene III proclaimed a Second Crusade. A summary of the massacres follows:

The Jews of Wurtzburg, Germany; of Cologne, Germany; of Bachrach, Germany, were massacred.

1168 A.D., Blood libel in Gloucester, England.

1171 A.D., Fifty-one Jews were burned at the stake in Blois, France.

1181 A.D., Jews were seized in Paris while attending Sabbath services and held for ransom. Blood libel in Bury St. Edmunds England.

1182 A.D., Blood libel in Saragossa, Spain. Jews were expelled from part of France.

1189 A.D., Many Jews were killed in anti-Jewish riots in London, England.

1190 A.D., Third Crusade. The Jews of Norwich, England; of Stamfordfair, England; of York, England; of Bury St. Edmunds, England were massacred.

1192 A.D., Blood libel in Winchester, England.

1196 A.D., Fifteen Jews were killed in Vienna by participants of the Third Crusade.

1197 A.D., Many Jews in Neuss, France were killed.

1206 A.D., Jews in Halle, Germany were killed; the rest were expelled.

1209 A.D., Two hundred Jews were killed in a massacre in Beziers, Provence.

1211 A.D., Jews were imprisoned for ransom by the King of England.

1216 A.D., Pope Innocent III ordered Jews to wear a badge in order to distinguish them from the rest of the population.

1221 A.D., Many Jews were killed in Erfurt, Germany, in a massacre. The Jews of Sicily and Pisa were ordered to wear blue badges.

1225 A.D., The Jews were expelled from Cremona and Pavia, Italy.

1230 A.D., The Jews of Wiener-Neusadt, Austria were attacked by the anti-Jewish rioters for 11 days. Many Jews were killed. Many Jews were forced to convert to Christianity in Astorga, Spain.

1235 A.D., Seven Jews were tortured and burned at the stake in Bischofsheim, Germany. Thirty-four Jews were killed in Fulda, Germany in a blood libel.

1236 A.D., More than 2,500 Jews were killed in France by mobs.

1240 A.D., Pope Gregory IX ordered the confiscation of all copies of the Talmud and other Jewish books. The Jews were expelled from Brittany, France, by a local duke.

1241 A.D., Most of the Jews of Frankfort Am Main, Germany were massacred and the Jewish quarter was destroyed.

1242 A.D., The Jews of Spain were forced to attend conversion sermons by order of the king, James I or Aragon. Massive burning of the Talmud took place in Paris, France.

1243 A.D., Jews in Belitz, Germany, were burned to death. First recorded libel of ritual desecration. (The charge, called "desecration of the host" said that Jews purposely desecrated one of the Christian sacraments. The Catholic Church teaches that the communion wafer literally becomes the body of Christ and that the wine literally becomes His blood. It was believed that Jews would sneak into churches and steal the wafer and the wine and then desecrate it in their rituals thus desecrating Christ.) Eleven Jews were killed in a blood libel in Kitzingen, Germany.

1247 A.D., Emperor Frederick II had planned to kill all the Jews in his Holy Roman Empire if the blood libel in Fulda (1235) were true. Upon much investigation, he concluded that blood libels were false. Pope Innocent IV also stated that the blood libels were false. In that same year, many Jews in Valreas, France were tortured, mutilated, and killed in a blood libel.

1248 A.D., Christians were forbidden to have contact with Jews.

1253 A.D., Many Jews were killed in Lincoln, England in a blood libel.

1255 A.D., Jews of Rome were required to wear a special badge.

1257 A.D., Jews of Mainz, Germany were required to wear a special badge.

1259 A.D., Jews of Amstadt, Germany were attacked and massacred by anti-Jewish rioters.

1265 A.D., Twenty Jews were killed in Koblenz, Germany.

1266 A.D., Twelve Jews were killed in Cologne, Germany. Jews were required to wear special hats in parts of Poland.

1269 A.D., Jews of France were ordered to wear special badge.

1275 A.D., Jews were expelled from Worchester, England.

1277 A.D., Jews were attacked in an anti-Jewish riot in Pamplona, Spain and their houses destroyed.

1278 A.D., Pope Nicholas III issued an order that Jews must attend conversion sermons by Christian priests. Jews of England were subjected to very restrictive laws as to where they could live and what they could do for work, and were forced to pay very high taxes.

1279 A.D., Many Jews were killed in London in a blood libel.

1281 A.D., Jews were killed in a blood libel in Mainz, Germany and a synagogue burned.

1283 A.D., Another blood libel occurred and many Jews were killed in ensuing massacres.

1285 A.D., One hundred and eighty Jews were killed in a blood libel in Munich, Germany.

1286 A.D., Forty Jews were killed in a blood libel in Oberwesel, Germany.

1287 A.D., Massacre of Jews in Bachrach, Germany.

1288 A.D., Thirteen Jews were burned at the stake by the Inquisition in Troyes, France in a blood libel. Others were killed in a blood libel in Neuchatel, Switzerland.

1289 A.D., Jews were expelled from Anjou and Le Mans, France.

1290 A.D., England forced Jews to leave the country. Jews of Naples, Bari, and other Italian cities were massacred in a blood libel.

1294 A.D., Jews were killed in Berne, Switzerland in a blood libel.

1298-1303 A.D., The Rindfleisch massacres of Rottingen, Germany began. As many as 100,000 deaths occurred over the ensuing years as the massacre spread to some 150 Jewish communities.

1306 A.D., Jews were expelled from France.

1309 A.D., One hundred ten Jews were killed by a mob in Born, Netherlands and many were killed after refusing to be baptized in Louvain, Belgium.

1312 A.D., Many Jews were killed in Fuerstenfeld and Judenberg, Austria in a ritual desecration libel and a blood libel.

1319 A.D., Several Jews were burned at the stake in Tudela, Spain.

1320 A.D., More than 500 Jews were killed in the Pastoreaux Crusades. Jews were expelled from Milan, Italy.

1321 A.D., One hundred sixty Jews were burned at the stake in France on a charge of poisoning wells in Chinon, in Vitry, and in Tours.

1322 A.D., Jews were expelled in parts of France.

1326 A.D., Twenty-seven Jews were killed in a ritual desecration in Constance, Germany.

1328 A.D., Six thousand Jews were killed in anti-Jewish riots in the province of Navarre, Spain.

1332 A.D., Three hundred Jews were killed in a blood libel in Uberlingen, Germany when a mob set a synagogue on fire.

1336 A.D., Over one thousand five hundred Jews were killed as bands of peasants who wore arm-bands roamed over Germany for three years and ravaged 120 Jewish communities.

1337 A.D., Many Jews were killed in massacres in Bohemia.

1349 A.D., The Black Death killed thousands of Jews over the ensuing years as Jews were blamed for the deaths of as much as half of the total population of Europe.

1367 A.D., The Jews of Barcelona, Spain were accused of ritual desecration; three Jews were killed and all the Jews were held prisoner in a synagogue for three days.

1377 A.D., Some Jews of Huesca, Spain were tortured and burned to death in a ritual desecration libel.

1389 A.D., Three thousand Jews were killed in Prague, their houses burned and their cemetery desecrated.

1391 A.D., Four thousand Jews were killed in Seville, Spain. The massacre spread throughout Spain and Portugal killing a total of 50,000 Jews.

1393 A.D., The Jews of Venice were required to wear a yellow badge.

1394 A.D., The final expulsion of Jews from France occurred.

1397 A.D., The Jews were expelled from Basel, Switzerland.

1400 A.D., Seventy-seven Jews were killed in anti-Jewish riots in Prague.

1401 A.D., Thirty Jews were burned at the stake in a blood libel in Schaffhausen, Switzerland.

1404 A.D., Many Jews were killed in Salzburg, Austria in a ritual desecration libel.

1407 A.D., The Jews of Cracow were attacked by a riotous mob in a blood libel.

1421 A.D., The Jews of Austria were massacred in the Weiner Gezerz after a ritual desecration libel.

1424 A.D., The Jews were expelled from Cologne, Germany.

1426 A.D., The Jews were expelled from Iglau, Bohemia.

1427 A.D., The Jews were expelled from Berne, Switzerland.

1428 A.D., Fifteen Jews were expelled from Fribourg, Switzerland.

1430 A.D., Fifteen Jews were burned to death in a blood libel.

1436 A.D., The Jews were expelled from Zurich.

1442 A.D., The Jews were expelled from Upper Bavaria (Germany).

1446 A.D., The Jews were expelled from Berlin.

1449 A.D., Many Jews were expelled from 40 cities.

1451 A.D., Jews were forbidden to have social contact with non-Jews by order of Pope Nicholas V.

1453 A.D., Forty-one Jews were burned at the stake in Breslau, Silesia in a ritual desecration libel.

1454 A.D., Many Jews were killed in anti-Jewish riots in Cracow.

1457 A.D., The Jews were expelled from Hildesheim, Germany.

1458 A.D., The Jews were expelled from Erfurt, Germany.

1459 A.D., Sixty Jews were killed in anti-Jewish riots in Carpentras, France.

1460 A.D., The Jews were expelled from Mainz, Germany.

1464 A.D., The Jews were attacked in Seville, Spain in anti-Jewish riots. Thirty Jews were killed in anti-Jewish riots in Cracow.

1465 A.D., Many Jews were massacred in a revolt in Fez, Morocco.

1466 A.D., Some Jews were killed in Arnstadt, Germany and the rest expelled.

1467 A.D., Eighteen Jews were burned to death in a blood libel in Nuremburg, **Germany.**

1468 A.D., The Jews of Landau, Germany were forced to wear yellow badges.

1470 A.D., Three Jews were killed in a blood libel in Endigen, Germany. The rest were expelled from the whole province of Baden.

1472 A.D., The Jews were expelled from Schaffhausen, Switzerland. The Jews of Muehlhausen, Germany were required to wear yellow badges and were forbidden to enter non-Jewish houses.

1473 A.D., Jews were massacred in Cordova.

1474 A.D., Three hundred sixty Jews were killed in a massacre in Sicily and Segovia, Spain.

1475 A.D., Many Jews of Trent, Italy were tortured and killed in a blood libel. Some Jews were forcibly baptized and the rest were expelled.

1477 A.D., The Jews were expelled from Tuebingen, Germany. They were also ordered expelled from Nancy and the whole Duchy of Lorraine, France.

1478 A.D., Ten Jews were killed in a ritual desecration libel in Passau, Bavaria and the rest expelled. The Jews were expelled from Bamberg, Germany. There was a blood libel in Mantua, Italy.

1480 A.D., Three Jews were burned at the stake in a blood libel in Venice.

1485 A.D., The Jews were attacked in anti-Jewish riots in many towns of Provence (France) and many were killed. The Spanish Inquisition burned 22 Marranos (Jewish forced converts; "Marrano" was a derogatory name given to them and means "pig" or "Swine") in Perpignan, France.

1488 A.D., Sixteen Jews were burned at the stake in Toledo, Spain.

1489 A.D., The Jews were attacked in parts of Provence, France; some were forcibly converted and the rest ordered to leave.

1490 A.D., Four hundred and twenty-two Marranos were burned in Toledo.

1491 A.D., The Jews were expelled from Thurgau, Switzerland. Jews were expelled from Ravenna, Italy and the synagogue was burned.

1492 A.D., A Jew was burned at the stake in Avila, Spain on a blood libel and another was stoned to death by an angry mob. The Jews were expelled from Spain and Sicily. It is estimated that 100,000 to 300,000 Jews were expelled. Twenty-seven Jews were burned at the stake in Meklenburg, Germany in a ritual desecration libel.

1494 A.D., Sixteen Jews were killed in Tyrnau, Slovakia in a blood libel.

1495 A.D., Most of the Jews of Cosenza, Italy were forced to become baptized.

1496 A.D., The Jews were expelled from Portugal. The expulsion order gave them one year to either convert or leave the country.

1497 A.D., The government of Portugal brought 20,000 Jews to a Lisbon palace where they denied them food and water and forcibly baptized them.

1499 A.D., Seventy-five Marranos were burned at the stake in Avila, Spain.

1501 A.D., The Jews were expelled from Provence, France.

1502 A.D., A number of Jews were burned at the stake in Dubrovnik, Yugoslavia.

1504 A.D., The Jews were expelled from Pilsen, Bohemia in a ritual desecration libel.

1505 A.D., The Jews were expelled from Orange, France.

1506 A.D., Two thousand Marranos were killed in Lisbon. In Venice, Italy a Jew was stoned to death by an angry crowd in a blood libel.

1510 A.D., A rabbi was killed in Prague in a libel. Thirty-eight Jews were burned at the stake in Berlin in a ritual desecration libel.

1515 A.D., The Jews were expelled from Laibach, Slovenia and from Genoa.

1516 A.D., The Jews of Venice were ordered to move from the city to a restricted area where there had been a foundry (ghetto). The Jews were expelled from Lowicz, Poland.

1518 A.D., The Jews of Hevron were attacked. Many were killed.

1519 A.D., The Jews were expelled from the region of Weurtemberg, Germany and from Regensburg, Bavaria.

1525 A.D., The Jews of Carpentras, France were ordered by Pope Clement VII to wear yellow hats.

1526 A.D., The Jews were expelled from Hungary.

1529 A.D., Thirty Jews were burned to death in Poesing, Slovakia in a blood libel.

1530 A.D., The Jews of Germany were required to wear a yellow badge.

1533 A.D., The Jews were expelled from Constance, Germany.

1534 A.D., Many Jews were massacred in Tlemcen, Algeria when the Spanish conquered the town.

1537 A.D., Many Jews were killed in Tyrnau, Slovakia on a blood libel.

1541 A.D., The Jews were massacred in Bohemia after an order was issued expelling them from the country.

1542 A.D., The Jews of Kalisch, Poland were attacked in anti-Jewish riots.

1543 A.D., The Jews were expelled from Muehlhausen, Germany and other towns through the influence of Martin Luther.

1547 A.D., Many Jews were killed in Treviso, Italy in anti-Jewish riots and the rest left the town.

1551 A.D., The Jews in Austria were required to wear a yellow badge.

1553 A.D., Pope Julius II ordered the burning of the Talmud because of its alleged anti-Christian content.

1555 A.D., The Jews of Rome were ordered by Pope Paul IV to live in ghettos. Men were required to wear yellow hats and women yellow kerchiefs.

1556 A.D., Twenty-six Marranos who had openly returned to Judaism were burned to death in Ancona, Italy by order of Pope Paul IV.

1563 A.D., Thirty Jews of Polotzk, Lithuania were drowned in the Daugava River for refusing to be baptized.

1566 A.D., Jewish men were required to wear yellow hats in Lithuania and women were required to wear yellow kerchiefs.

1569 A.D., The Jews were expelled from the Papal States by Pope Pious V.

1577 A.D., Twenty Jews were killed in anti-Jewish riots in Posen, Poland. Pope Gregory XIII ordered the Jews of Rome and Ancona to attend conversion sermons in churches.

1590 A.D., Jews were expelled from Petrokov, Poland after a blood libel.

1605 A.D., The Jews in The Jews in Bisenz, Moravia were massacred.

1630 A.D., One Jew was killed in Przemysl, Poland in a ritual desecration libel. Eighteen Jewish children were forcibly baptized in Riggio Emilia, Italy. The Jews of Venice and of Prague were forced to attend Christian conversion sermons.

1635 A.D., The Jews of Vilna were attacked and their houses ransacked.

1639 A.D., The Jews of Lublin were attacked and some killed after a blood libel trial. Twenty Jews were arrested and tortured in a blood libel in Lunshitz, Poland. Two were later publicly killed in front of the synagogue and their bodies mutilated.

1648 A.D., Poland-Lithuania became a scene of massive destruction of Jewish people – 6,000 were killed in Nemirov; 1,000 were killed in Tulchin; 10,000 were killed in Polonye; 3,000 were killed in Staro-Konstantinov; 4,000 were killed in Dubno; 12,000 were killed in Narol; and 40,000 were killed in Narol, Poland.

1649 A.D., Ninety-six Marranos were burned to death in Mexico.

1650 A.D., Many Jews were killed in Jassy, Moldavia by the Cossacks.

1651 A.D., Many Jews were killed in Bar, Ukraine by the Cossacks and the Tartars.

1655 A.D., Most of the Jews of Sandomierz and Tamobrzeg, Poland were killed and the rest expelled.

1656 A.D., Three hundred and fifty Jewish families were killed in Krotoszyn, Poland by the Polish resistance in the war against Sweden. Two hundred families were killed in Apta; 100 families in Brest Kuyavzk; 50 families in Cheshanov; 40 families in Brzeziny; and 150 Jews in Checiny – all towns in Poland. Three thousand Jews were killed when the Polish recaptured Lunshitz, Poland.

1658 A.D., Three Jews were killed in Cracow.

1659 A.D., Hundreds of Jews were killed in Kalisch, Poland at the end of the war with Sweden. Eight Jews were killed in Przemysl, Poland. Rabbi Yisrael ben Shalom and Rabbi Tuvyah Bachrach were killed in Ruzhany, Poland in a blood libel. Three hundred Jews were killed in Bichov, Poland when the Russians captured the town.

1663 A.D., A Jewish physician was dismembered and burned in Cracow after being accused of cursing Christianity.

1670 A.D., A rabbi was burned to death on a blood libel charge in Metz, France.

1682 A.D., Many Jews were killed in Cracow in anti-Jewish riots.

1683 A.D., All the Jews of Uhersky Brod, Moravia were killed.

1704 A.D., The Jews of Krotoszyn, Poland were attacked and their property looted in anti-Jewish riots.

1706 A.D., The Jews of Lissa, Poland were attacked and plundered by invading Russian soldiers; the whole Jewish section of the town was burned.

1710 A.D., The Jews were expelled from Groningen, Netherlands.

1720 A.D., The Jews of Budapest were attacked and their homes plundered.

1726 A.D., The Jews were attacked in Jassy, Moldavia after a blood libel in Posen, Poland.

1736 A.D., Many Jews were imprisoned and tortured in a blood libel and the synagogues were desecrated.

1737 A.D., Some Jews were tortured and killed in a blood libel in Yaroslav, Poland.

1742 A.D., The Jews were expelled from most of what was then Russia.

1745 A.D., Some Jews were massacred in Roudnice, Bohemia. The Jews were expelled from Prague.

1746 A.D., The Jews were expelled from Budapest.

1747 A.D., Five Jews were killed in a blood libel in Izyaslav, Poland.

1753 A.D., Eleven Jews were skinned alive and then killed and 13 were forced to convert to Christianity in a blood libel in Zhitomir, Poland.

1755 A.D., A Jew was killed in Colmar, Alsace after a libel trial.

1761 A.D., Many Jews were killed in Mogilev-Podolski (then Poland) and some Jews of Wojslawice, Poland were killed in a blood libel.

1762 A.D., The Jews of Emden, Germany were attacked in anti-Jewish riots.

1763 A.D., Four Jews were killed in Kalisch, Poland in a blood libel.

1801 A.D., One hundred twenty-eight Jews were killed in anti-Jewish riots in Bucharest after a blood libel.

1804 A.D., A Russian edict prohibited Jews from living in villages.

1821 A.D., The Jews in Odessa, Russia were attacked in anti-Jewish riots.

1822 A.D., The expulsion of Jews from Russian villages was resumed.

1825 A.D., Jews were expelled from the villages around Mogilev and Vitebsk, Russia and removed to cities.

1829 A.D., The Jews were ordered expelled from Kiev and later from the Russian port cities of Nikolayev.

1867 A.D., The Jews were expelled from many villages in Rumania.

1871 A.D., The Jews were attacked in anti-Jewish riots in Odessa, Russia.

1881 A.D., Many Jews left Russia after a wave of pogroms.

1882 A.D., Some Jews were accused in a blood libel in Tisza Eszlar, Hungary.

1891 A.D., The Jews were expelled from Moscow, Russia; 30,000 were forced to see their properties and leave.

1897 A.D., Jews were attacked in a pogrom in Bucharest.

1899 A.D., Leopold Hilsner was sentenced to death in Bohemia in a blood libel. His sentence was later reduced to life imprisonment.

1903 A.D., Forty-nine Jews were killed and 500 were injured in Kishinev, Russia in a pogrom which had begun with a blood libel. Eigt Jews were killed in Homel, Russia in a pogrom and 36 of the Jews who fought in self-defense were charged with committing a pogrom against Russian citizens.

1905 A.D., More than 800 Jews were killed over the course of less than two years after almost 700 sanctioned pogroms were carried out against them.

1915 A.D., A Jew, Leo Frank, who had been charged with murder based upon flimsy evidence, was lynched by an anti-Semitic mob in Georgia, in the United States.

1918 A.D., Over 60,000 Jews were killed over the next two years as a result of pogroms in Russia.

1933-1945 A.D., At this time we begin to see the mass persecution and ultimately the destruction of 6 million Jews in Europe by the Nazis, who had just come to power at that time. Needless to say, this Holocaust is well-documented and attested to by many books and historians; so much so that the pages of this small book could not even hold all the records of atrocities conducted during the Holocaust. I do not wish to minimize the importance or severity of this persecution, but to acknowledge it as the most horrendous act of satanic barbarism ever perpetrated upon the Jewish people.

Proof that anti-Semitism is satanically inspired is in the multitudes of nations that have sanctioned and condoned it within their borders. It is not a sickness of just one nation or religion, rather, it crosses all religions and nations: England, France, Italy, Germany, Poland, Lithuania, Russia and many others which is indicative that a higher power then mankind is at work.

Conclusion

Perhaps you have just had your eyes opened for the first time to the mass atrocities that were directed against the Jewish people throughout the centuries. I expect you feel disgust and anger toward those who would do such things against any people.

Nevertheless, such anti-Semites are still around (some disguised as Christian groups). If they are left unchecked, they will continue to propagate their satanic lies and destruction against the Jewish people.

Pseudo-Christian groups such as the Posse Comitatus, the New Order, the Christian Defense League, the Ku Klux Klan, the Sword and Arm of the Lord and Aryan Nations in this country exist and flourish, blaming the current economic condition of this country upon the Jews. A group called Pomyat in the former Soviet Union also flourishes for the same reason and proclaims the same message.

All it takes for these groups to grow unchecked is for people who know better – like you – to remain silent. Hopefully this chapter will spur you to take an active role against such lies, to counter them with truth.

Perhaps when Christians have an understanding of the world's past dealings with the Jews they will develop a sensitivity toward Israel and the Jewish people. Perhaps then they will stand up for the Jews when atrocities threaten, even when doing so could risk their own lives and well-being.

Chapter Five

To Tell the Truth

It is said that the best way to counter a lie is to respond with truth. Nevertheless, it is a fact that not everyone will believe the truth, or act upon it, when they hear it. Regardless of the way the listener responds, though, the truth must be spoken.

Jesus said, "I am the way, the truth, and the life" (John 14:6 NAS). You would think that everyone would be interested in knowing the truth. Yet when Pilate asked Jesus, "What is truth?" he wasn't willing to listen to the "truth" even though it was standing right before him.

In fact, some people get downright angry when presented with the truth because they would rather be in darkness, that their evil might not be seen.

[19] "This is the judgment, that the Light has come into the world, and men loved the darkness rather than the Light, for their deeds were evil. [20] "For everyone who does evil hates the Light, and does not come to the Light for fear that his deeds will be

exposed. [21] "But he who practices the truth comes to the Light, so that his deeds may be manifested as having been wrought in God." (John 3 NAS)

It is up to the righteous of the world to practice and preach the truth even though it is not popular in the eyes of our fellow man. I believe this is what Jesus meant when He said we are to be salt in this world (Matthew 5:13). Salt is a preservative and a flavoring agent. When placed upon meat, it prevents the meat from spoiling. The world would slip into eternal hell much faster without believers being sprinkled into the midst of the nations, proclaiming truth.

However many believers are in danger of losing, and indeed have lost their flavor as this verse in Matthew states. They have compromised with the world and allowed the world's standards to replace the standards set by God. They are then good for nothing and are indeed trampled under the foot of man.

Look at how pastors and Christians are portrayed on television today. Why is it that way? It is because so many Christians have compromised in their faith and let the world determine their values that they have lost their flavor. Thus the world is either spitting them out or absorbing them.

Today's world standards are not fixed by some higher authority, they are humanistic and relative-oriented. In other words, "If it feels good, do it."

The state, society or humanism sets the standards – not God. This is the standard by which Hitler, Stalin and Mao Tse Tung justified the killing of millions of people. What was good for the state or society was good for the people.

It is time for believers to hear the call to action. We need to get off our spiritual derrieres, get out of our own materialistic, relative world, and get back to pleasing God. This means we do what He says and not what the world says. Going to church once a week and "putting in your time for the Big Man" won't cut it; especially *if the life that claims to be Christian isn't living like one for the rest of the week*. The Epistle of James states that a faith without works is dead (2:26). The evidence that a believer has true saving faith is the works that faith naturally produces. If we are true believers, the Holy Spirit *will* produce fruit in our lives (Galatians 5:22-25). One of these fruits is love.

Love means not simply just loving those who love you and agree with you, but like the parable of the Good Samaritan in Luke 10:30-37 explains, it means loving those who are being exploited. The Scriptures say that we are not to be hearers only, but also doers (Luke 6:46-49; cf. James 1:22-24).

When atrocities or persecution in any form occur against any people, we need to speak up – not bury our heads like frightened ostriches and pretend such things aren't happening. If we mobilize and unite, we will speak with a power and authority that the Enemy cannot stand against. Remember this: we are not fighting against flesh and blood, but "against the rulers, against the powers, against the world forces of this darkness, against the spiritual forces of wickedness in the heavenly places" (Ephesians 4:12).

If we do nothing, evil men will have their way.

I sometimes wonder if we as believers have learned the lessons of the Holocaust? Racial cleansing is happening all over the world. Are we saying anything?

Are we calling and writing our governmental leaders to let them know what we wish to see done by the United States in this matter? Or are we apathetic to what is occurring there because it doesn't affect us or we are too busy with other things in our lives?

Yet, even if human help is not available, we need to remember that with only one believer and God, we have a majority in the battle against the Enemy.

When surrounded by enemies who threatened their lives, Elisha's servant cried in fear, "Alas, my master! What shall we do?" What was Elisha's response? "Do not fear, for those who are with us are more than those who are with them." Elisha then prayed that his servant's eyes be opened. The Lord opened the servant's eyes to see that they were surrounded by a vast army of the heavenly host (2 Kings 6:8-23).

The persecution of the Jewish people is not a simple flesh and blood issue either. It is Satan's last ditch effort to prevent the Second Coming of Jesus!

If you are a true believe in Him, you should be concerned! If there are no Jews to utter the words to usher Him back, He will not come back!

Do you want Him to come back? Stand then for His people!

Fortunately, we know the end of the story: He does come back and there are Jews in Jerusalem who utter these words when they are surrounded by their enemies and there is no one to help but God! Read Zechariah chapters 12-14.

Woe to the believer who aides and abets the enemy by helping the enemy carry out his plot to prevent the King of Kings and the Lord of Lords from returning!

Chapter Six

To Respond to the Lies...

Christians need the true facts in order to respond to the lies against the Jewish people. How can a person rebuke a liar unless the lie is thrown into the light and the truth discovered?

In this chapter, I shall bring some of these lies to light and help you prepare a response to them when they come up in conversation about Jewish people.

Blood Libel

Blood libel is a lie that says that the Jewish people use a Christian child's blood during their rituals, particularly Passover.

If you are familiar with Scripture, you can see how ridiculous this is. Jews are very conscious of observing the biblical kosher laws of Leviticus 11 – particularly that of abstaining from eating blood (Leviticus 17:11).

The best response to this lie is to say that Jews do not eat blood and the Torah expressly forbids them from doing so. The Torah also abhors the pagans who eat blood and who sacrifice children. Although the nations surrounding Israel did so, they themselves were commanded not to use blood in this manner.

Ritual Desecration

During the period of heavy Catholic rule in temporal matters, it was believed that the Jewish people would steal into churches and remove the elements of the Lord's Table (communion) so the Jews might desecrate them in their ceremonies. It is believed by Catholics that the wine and bread wafer actually become the blood and body of Christ. It was said that by ritually desecrating the host (the bread) and pounding a nail through it, the Jewish people were once again crucifying Christ.

The best response to this view is to point out that there is absolutely no historical, factual basis that Jewish people actually ever did this. "Confessions" made under duress of torture do not establish that such practices occur.

The Protocols of the Elders of Zion

In the reign of Czar Nicholas II, anti-Semitism in Russia rose to its greatest heights. The Czar gave money to the anti-Semitic organization called "The Black Hundreds" and made no secret about his personal membership in the organization. This organization was associated with the government in directly inciting pogroms against the Jewish people from 1903 to 1905.

It was in 1905 that the "Protocols" were published under the auspices of the Czar's secret police and by his press, although the Czar believed the work to be a fraud, after much investigation.

The "Protocols" are purported to be the guidebook to a Jewish conspiracy to take over the world. If fixes the blame for any and every problem of a nation on the Jewish people.

In czarist Russia it was used to make the Jew the scapegoat for a corrupt and discredited government after Russia's defeat at the hands of the Japanese. The Nazis likewise used it to explain Germany's depression after her bitter defeat by the Allies in World War I.

In 1921 a correspondent of the London Times found that half of the "Protocols" were a plagiarism from the satire on Napoleon III written by Maurice Joly, a French attorney.

The best response to this fictitious work is to respond that it is neither a Jewish document nor the framework for a Jewish conspiracy to take over the world. Instead, it is a work produced by the Czar to fix the blame for his corrupt government upon someone else. Even he knew it wasn't true!

It was to be proven a blatant hoax by the Berne trial in 1935...even so, Hitler and others have used this same fictitious work to fix the blame for their country's problems upon someone else.

With our sinful human nature, it is always easier to fix the blame for our problems on someone else than to "fess up to it" and shoulder the blame ourselves or to pinpoint the real culprits. Governments do this all the time when things go wrong economically, politically, or socially.

If there is really a conspiracy of Jews to take over the world, why aren't most Jews benefitting from it? Most of the Jewish people are no better off than those people who are not Jewish.

That the Jews killed Christ

The greatest lie in the Adversary's arsenal to promote violence and slander against the Jewish people is this one: that the Jews rejected and killed Christ.

Granted, many Jewish people (especially among the Jewish leadership of that day) rejected Jesus, but that does not give credence in any way to the statement that all Jewish people rejected Him. In fact, many accepted Him as Messiah! Acts 21:20 tells us that there were "myriads of believers" in Jesus (His Hebrew name is "Yeshua") among the Jewish people – and this is by approximately 58-60 A.D.! The Greek word says that there were literally "tens of thousands" of Messianic Jews!

So, to imply that ALL the Jewish people rejected Jesus is a lie from Hell! And the early Greek Church Fathers bought into in "hook, line and sinker."

A misconception promoted in the early Gentile church said that the Jews (implying all of them) rejected and crucified Him. Passages in the New Testament Scriptures, such as those found in Matthew 27:20-25, Mark 15:8-15, Luke 23:13-25 and John 19:1-16 are used by them as "proof texts" to support this view.

However, recent archaeological discoveries show that in Pilate's Praetorium only several hundred people (at best) could fit into this area. Therefore, when it seems that a multitude of Jewish people wanted to see Jesus killed, it was actually only a few hundred who were there and called for "His blood" to be "upon us and our children."

The significance of this is: although it is true that the Jewish people assembled in that courtyard that morning wanted to see Jesus killed, this group hardly represented the position of the Jewish people at large, who at that time were still probably in bed.

Would it be fair to say that the United States of America is a "Gay Nation" because 300,000 homosexuals marched in Washington, D.C.? What about the position of the other some 300 million other Americans? Should we lump their position into that of the 300,000 vocally gay Americans demonstrating in the Mall that day? Hardly! So, why do we say that the entire Jewish populace wanted Jesus killed?

The Scriptures say that the multitudes outside that courtyard gave great consideration to Jesus! John 7:25-32, 40-53 says that "many of the multitude believed in Him" (v. 31 NAS). In fact, many of the rulers also believed in Him (John 12:42-43)!

You don't hear the anti-Semites quoting those Scriptures! Nope. They've bought into the Satanic lie from the pit of Hell and many of them will be following Satan to that pit.

The most obvious reason that Jesus' "trial" occurred illegally at night was so that those rulers and leaders who did believe in Him wouldn't get in the way of those who wanted to see Him dead!

There were so many believers in Jesus amongst the Jews that John 12:19 records, "the whole world has gone after Him (NAS)."

Not only were there multitudes of Jewish believers before His crucifixion, there were also multitudes after His crucifixion and resurrection! On the Day of Pentecost, 3,000 Jewish people were baptized. How do I know they were Jewish?

I know this from the passage in Acts 2:5-10. The only ones there were Jews and Jewish converts (proselytes). There wasn't a Gentile (outside of the converted ones to Judaism) in the lot! Furthermore, Acts 4:4 says that 5,000 Jewish people came to the Lord later. Then there were more: "multitudes of men and women were constantly added to their number" (Acts 5:14 NAS).

It would not be until Cornelius met with Peter (roughly 10 years later) that the first non-Jewish convert would come into the faith (Acts 10).

You see, it was not a "we" versus "they" issue as the anti-Semites portray it. It wasn't the "Christians" against those "Jews!" It was Jew against Jew. Jesus is a Jew (He still is the Lion of Judah); His disciples were all Jews; His first follower were Jews; and the first congregations of the Messiah consisted of all Jews and Jewish converts.

It would not be until Acts 11:26 that the first non-Jewish congregation in Antioch would be formed. That's a full 10 years AFTER the death and resurrection of Jesus.

Let's not make this issue something that it's not! Let's not fall for the plot of the Adversary of us all!

Now, did the Jews actually kill Christ Jesus?

No. For several reasons: the first is that those who arrested Him, tried Him and condemned Him that night were from the minority in Israel who feared that all the people would go after Him and the Romans would take away their kingdom.

Second, although this trial determined that Jesus was worthy of death for blasphemy (Matthew 14:64) it was unable to condemn Him because only Rome had jurisdiction over death sentences in the lands they conquered.

So even though the process was instigated by many of the Jewish leaders it required non-Jewish complicity to carry the death sentence to its conclusion.

Note how the charges against Jesus during His trial were religious. If Israel were able to put a man to death, it would have been justified by Scripture on those grounds alone.

Yes, Israel was not able to put a man to death under Roman rule, and at the time Rome would not kill a man of Israel for breaking a Jewish religious law! So the chief priests and elders brought Jesus up before Pilate on political charges (Mark 15:2). There was no other king but Caesar, or those in kingship under Caesar's authority, and anyone violating this Roman law was subject to death.

Even though Pilate could not find fault with Jesus (Matthew 27:24; Luke 23:13-14), he released Him to be crucified because the chief priests implied that it would get back to Caesar if he released this "king" who "opposes Caesar" (John 19:12 NAS).

It was actually the soldiers of the Governor who took Him from there and actually crucified Him (Matthew 27:27-37). From that point on, the Jewish people, guilty or otherwise, could only look on.

Now, when we ask the question again, "Who actually killed Jesus?" The answer for a certainty is, "It was the Gentiles who actually killed Him!"

But the complicity for the death of Jesus actually goes even farther: flesh and blood alone did not bear sole responsibility for the death of Jesus. Jesus Himself bore the responsibility for His own death! He said that He alone had the authority to lay down His life. No one could take that away from Him (John 10:17-18). If He didn't want to die, there was no power on earth or in Heaven who could make Him.

The authority that Pilate had to crucify Jesus came from above; it was God-ordained (John 19:11). Even Pilate couldn't kill Jesus unless Heaven was part of His crucifixion. If Jesus wanted to stop it, He had only to say the word and His servants would be fighting (John 18:36). In fact, He could have called twelve legions of angels to save Him (Matthew 26:53).

If you read what damage a single angel could do to the earth and its inhabitants (read Revelation 16:1-21) you will quickly come to the conclusion that if Jesus did not want to be arrested, tried, or crucified, then He had ample power at His disposal to prevent it anywhere along the line!

You see, what Jesus went through was actually a plan from Heaven to redeem mankind from sin (Hebrews 1:14; 2:9-15; 5:7-9; 7:25-27; 9:11-28; 10:4-10).   Heaven was a necessary part of the crucifixion of Jesus – if it hadn't been, His death would never have happened.

But, it was because "God so loved the world, that He gave His only begotten Son, that whoever believes in Him should not perish, but have eternal life (John 3:16)."

He died not because of the Jews alone, or the Gentiles alone, but because of all of us! If it weren't for our sins, He would never have had to die!

Did the Jews kill Jesus? Yes. Did the Gentiles kill Jesus? Yes. We ALL killed Jesus because we all sinned and deserved to die, but He died instead of us, as a substitute for us (1 John 2:1-2)!

Let's not lay the death of Christ solely at the feet of the Jews, but also at the feet of the Gentiles, at Himself and at Heaven! ALL of us had a part in His death!

So, when anti-Semitic people spout off their ignorance and say that the "Jews killed Jesus" remind them that they also played a part in Jesus' death. Not only that, but show them how Jesus, the Father and the angels played a part in the death of Jesus, too.

If Jesus didn't want to die, no one could have forced Him. He chose to die because He loves us and wants to provide a way to Heaven for all sinners, both Jew and Gentile alike!

Lies Concerning Israel and the Palestinians

Instead of my reinventing the wheel, let me recommend a most revealing booklet authored by Dr. Frank Eiklor entitled, *"Israel Front Page: The Untold Story,"* available from Shalom International, PO Box 310, Corona, CA 91718. Suffice it to say, don't believe most of what you hear or read through the liberal media regarding Israel and the Palestinians.

You are not getting the whole story from the mainstream media! In fact, there is so much bias against Israel in the media that you can hardly come away from reading a newspaper or watching the news on television without picking up on that anti-Semitic bias.

There IS a plot behind that bias (which this book is all about, and which hopefully you have picked up on by now) and it smells like smoke (from Hell, that is). The plot is exposed in Zechariah 12:2-3. Jerusalem will become a heavy stone for all the peoples, and all the nations will be gathered against Israel over the fate of the city. This is when the Battle of Armageddon will be fought to try to destroy the Jewish people once and for all (Zechariah 12:4-11; 14:1-5; cf. Revelation 16:14-16; 19-21)!

Fortunately, it is also the time that the Jewish people in Jerusalem shall cry out the words, "Blesse is He who comes in the name of the Lord"! Then our Lord shall return with power and great glory to defend Israel against her enemies and bring the nations to judgment for what they did to her throughout history (Joel 33:6-26; Amos 9:11-15; Zechariah 14:7-21).

In the long and short of it: the anti-Semites lose. So, why be on the losing side?

Now is the time to side with the greatest Jew of all on behalf of His people who He has chosen!

Chapter Seven

The Greatest Form of anti-Semitism

After reading this book, you would think that the greatest form of anti-Semitism has already been expressed here somewhere.

After all, what form of anti-Semitism could be greater than the Holocaust, in which more than six million Jewish people perished? Or what could be worse than the millennia of persecution, murder, pogroms, and lies that the Jewish people have endured? Surely, there isn't a form of anti-Semitism greater than all these?

Sadly enough, there is. The greatest form of anti-Semitism that exists is that of not sharing the true gospel of life with a Jewish person. Romans 1:16 says that "...the gospel... is the power of God for salvation to everyone who believes, to the Jew first and also to the Greek."

If Jesus is really the Messiah that Israel has been looking to for salvation, then the words that He uttered are just as true for the Jewish people as they are for the rest of the world. He said:

"I said therefore to you, that you shall die in your sins for unless you believe that I am He, you shall die in your sins." (John 8:24 NAS)

"I am the resurrection and the life; he who believes in Me shall live even if he dies, and everyone who lives and believes in Me shall never die." (John 11:25-26 NAS)

"I am the way, and the truth and the life; no one comes to the Father, but through Me." (John 14:6 NAS)

The greatest form of anti-Semitism is to let the Jewish people die in their sins without knowing the One who can forgive them of those sins; the One who made the perfect atonement for them with His blood.

We must share the gospel in love, not in the forced conversions and compulsions of the Church of the past. We love even as the Messiah loved – because we are His Body. The Jewish people need to know the joy, peace and love that comes with being a believer in Jesus, too.

As you have known the love of the Jewish Messiah, so go out and share that love with your Jewish friends until you've shown them what being a true Christian is all about.

Love the people through whom your Lord and Savior chose to be born through.

www.ingramcontent.com/pod-product-compliance
Lightning Source LLC
Chambersburg PA
CBHW070157290526
45789CB00002B/809